Lion Brothers

Lion Brothers

Winner of the 2017 Press 53 Award for Poetry

Leona Sevick

Press 53
Winston-Salem

Press 53, LLC
PO Box 30314
Winston-Salem, NC 27130

First Edition

A Tom Lombardo Poetry Selection

Copyright © 2017 by Leona Sevick

All rights reserved, including the right of reproduction in whole or in part in any form except in the case of brief quotations embodied in critical articles or reviews. For permission, contact publisher at editor@Press53.com, or at the address above.

Cover design by Kevin Morgan Watson

Author photo by Julie Napear
julienapearphotography.com

Printed on acid-free paper
ISBN 978-1-941209-52-3

For my mother and father

Grateful acknowledgment is made to the editors of the following publications who first published versions of these poems, sometimes under different titles:

ArLiJo: "Burn the Ships," "Self-help," and "Wishing Doll"
Barrow Street: "In Other News"
Bateau: "Law-man"
The Delaware Poetry Review: "Cow," "Pre-op," and "What I Learned from Ruby"
The Florida Review: "Heavier"
Frontiers: A Journal of Women Studies: "Lion Brothers"
Hawaii Pacific Review: "I'll Take Your Jacket When You Die"
The Journal: "Chink"
Lighted Corners: "News of the World"
Memoir Journal: "Three on the Tree"
Naugatuck River Review: "Not the Voice of God to Save Him"
North American Review: "Reconciliation"
Orange Coast Review: "The Corpse of Memory" and "When She Dies"
Poet Lore: "Meet the Faces"
Potomac Review: "Zoonosis" and "Any Dog Will Bite"
Quiddity: "Woodcutting"
Slippery Elm: "Mother"
Slipstream: "I Had Pretty Plumage Once"
Tar River Poetry: "Driving Home on a Cold Night after a Snow Storm"

"A Love Story" appears in *The Golden Shovel Anthology*. University of Arkansas Press, 2017.
"Bad Day" appears in *Chronicles of Eve*. Paper Swans Press, 2016.
"Clean" appears in *All We Can Hold: A Collection of Poetry on Motherhood*. Sage Hill Press, 2016.
"Cutaway" appears in *Circe's Lament: Anthology of Wild Women Poetry*, Accents Publishing, 2015.
"White" was chosen by Naomi Shihab Nye as the winner of the 2012 Split this Rock Poetry Contest.
Several poems appeared first in the chapbook *Damaged Little Creatures* (FutureCycle Press, 2015).

Contents

Introduction by Tom Lombardo	xi
Lion Brothers	1
Gun Safe	2
In Other News	3
Gangster Mad	4
Garage Door	5
I Had Pretty Plumage Once	6
When My Monster Finally Appeared	7
Tiger	8
Three on the Tree	9
Burn the Ships	10
The Corpse of Memory	11
Cutaway	12
OCD	13
Washing Rice	14
Dangerous Rooms	16
Wishing Doll	17
When I Leave You	18
Law-man	19
Amnesty	20
What I Learned from William James	21
Self-Help	22
Reconciliation	23
What I Learned from Ruby	24
When She Dies	25
Take You Back	26
White	27
Secure in Place	28
Something New	29
Heavier	30
Glamour Moving	31
Pre-op	32
Meet the Faces	33
Driving Home on a Cold Night after a Snow Storm	34
News of the Day	35

How to Talk to Strangers	36
1985	37
On the Anniversary of Your Infidelity	38
Cow	39
Not for the Voice of God to Save Him	40
The Transitive Property	41
Conditional Love	42
Notification of Family, 3 a.m.	43
Clean	44
Maybe Next Time	45
Woodcutting	46
Zoonosis	47
Wait for It	48
I'll Take Your Jacket When You Die	49
Any Dog Will Bite	50
It's No Wonder We Never Learned to Swim	51
Chink	52
Bad Day	53
Loaner	54
A Love Story	55
Mother	56
Go There	58
Acknowledgments	61
Author biography	63

Introduction

Once again, as poetry series editor for Press 53, I had the honor to read and consider all 315 entries in the annual Press 53 Award for Poetry. After winnowing the submissions down to a small group of finalists, I selected the collection you hold in your hands, Leona Sevick's *Lion Brothers*, as the award winner for 2017. The poems in *Lion Brothers* excited me with their high levels of emotion delivered in a clear and compelling voice. Using distinct diction and figuration in a pleasing flow, Sevick presents stories freshly, with stunning surprises, while maintaining strong connections between readers and the world. This collection holds together strongly with its overarching narrative that illuminates the dark corners of domestic life. Its poems show how family life in contemporary America can break to pieces. Under the right circumstances, there may be redemption, but under the wrong circumstances, there may be disaster that tears into the fabric of society.

The collection's title comes from the name of the textile factory in Taneytown, Maryland, where the poet's mother—a Korean immigrant—climbs giant looms with her tool belt tied around her slender waist, "her arms…knotted in muscles." Her co-workers call her "chink." The mother's fearless grit pushes her daughter "to find your own way…Right words. Right work. Right man. Right way," and those threads drive the collection's tension, irony, figuration.

In one poem, a couple under stress fight "over scratches on the fender and what to feed / the kids. Spent money and dishes stacked in the sink." When her husband mounts a ladder to do some needed maintenance, the wife "almost wish[es] you wouldn't fall." After all, what is a husband good for if not for "fixing the garage door that breaks down for the fourth time this month."

The issue of infidelity echoes across generations. A child hears his father's words to his mother: "I have something to tell you." Years later, a grown woman hears those same words from her own husband, leading to a breakup. Yet the woman takes him back: "Just when I think I can live without you…I think of / neck-snapped mice in complex traps…that box too heavy to lift squats on the landing / of my inadequacy…pave[s] the way for your return / and the sound of your breathing beside me."

Sevick offers domestic tension on a platter for the reader to experience a menu of emotions that whipsaw from tragedy to comedy and back to tragedy. At times, it may seem like "we burn our ships…ablaze behind us" like Cortés, and yet at other times, there may be quenching waters to douse the fires.

Sevick skillfully weaves poems about her own parents' hardscrabble blue-collar lives with poems about her assimilated, white-collar life. The issues seem to be different in the literal, but in the figurative they may be the same: personal values, love, transgression, raising children. At their roots, these poems are about survival in American domestic life. Sometimes it's beautiful, sometimes ugly, sometimes murderously violent. But it seems to come down to this:

> And afterward, poking through the smoking
> ash heap of this conflagration,
> I will search for remnants of my humanity
> I might salvage, still.

If you enjoy your "coffee, strong and black," as Sevick does, relax into your comfy chair with a cup and her collection. You're in for a great set of poems.

Tom Lombardo
Press 53 Poetry Series Editor

Lion Brothers

Sometimes they sent her home early,
her hand bandaged tight where a needle
had pierced her. Home from school,
I found her curled on the floor, watching.

She woke early to put on her face
before we could see it for what it
wasn't, round and smooth and yellow.
Her legs tucked under her,
she held the mirror in her tiny hand
and painted on the jungle colors:
blacks and blues. At the factory
she tied tools around her waist,
slimmer than any boy's though her arms
were knotted in muscles. She climbed up
beside the men, four feet above the ground
on their vibrating monsters, machines
that worked like animals. Like pieces
of thread cut from the loom and dropped
clean, their words gathered around her feet.

Chink.

Gun Safe

My father wore a gun on his ankle
wherever he went, even to church.
I told you it was because of his job,
because he never knew when he'd
have to save a life or to take one.
He taught me how to disengage
the safety, how to steady the surprising
weight of any gun in my hands
while I breathe out slowly, pull the trigger,
listen for the explosion and feel the kick
without blinking. The smell of gun oil
as familiar to me as coffee, I said
I never want one in my home;
we should live without one
because others say they can't.

I am alone, and the house, ordinarily
as quiet as old bones, comes alive.
The dog barks at no one and nothing
as he stares into his reflection
on the paneled windows along the sides
of the front door. And the shadows
that the hall tree stamps on the floor
make me feel like there's someone
standing there, even though I know
there isn't. The code to the gun safe
is in my head, burned there by years
of knowing the digits of your
birthday: the year, month, the day
your mother pushed you into this world.

It's a dangerous gift, knowing
what others want. Not the things
they say they want, but what is hidden
in the dark, deep pulse of blood, tucked
into the heavy folds of muscle and
complex valves where no one ever looks.

In Other News

Though Rothko has been dead
for as many years as I've been alive,
I guess I care how he'll take
this latest blow.

In London, a thug with a spray can
defaced a painting in his Seagram series,
one dark gathering of lines
spoiled by another's.

In other news, a mother of five glued
her small child to the wall and beat her senseless,
the grandmother weeping out her testimony
in open court.

Wanting consolation, I looked for my husband.
Water spitting into my face over the shower doors,
I shouted, *Can you believe someone would do that
to a Rothko?*

Gangster Mad

Slapping together a peanut butter and jelly
sandwich on bread I know I shouldn't eat,
I think how little it takes to push us over
the edge. In this world of tested hearts,
each fragile enough to balance on the rim
of a glass of Hendrick's gin, we may break.

Your mother? Dead. Your father? Dead. Your
pig-nosed daughter? Dead. Your foul dog,
your ficus plants, your vegetable garden all Dead.
Your brick rancher with all your hideous clothes
and stupid knick-knacks, burned to the ground.

And afterward, poking through the smoking
ash heap of this conflagration,
I will search for remnants of my humanity
I might salvage, still.

Garage Door

Caressing old wounds, we explore a catalog
of grievances one syllable at a time. We fight

over scratches on the fender and what to feed
the kids. Spent money and dishes stacked in the sink.

Who will scrub the toilet, then let the dog out?
And why does your mother talk to me that way?

Just then, the garage door breaks for the fourth time
this month. Here we are again, our throats thick

with accusations. You climb out of the car and walk
inside. I watch you spread the ladder's legs far enough

to support your hulking frame. And as you balance
on your good shoes, the ones you like so much,

I almost wish you wouldn't fall.

I Had Pretty Plumage Once

The bees alighting on clover so near my toes
have no interest in what I have to offer.
Fat wolf spiders on my porch jump at flies
and leave my arms, my legs, unmolested.
Unnamed snakes that could be copperheads,
but probably aren't, have no business here,
their forked tongues and fist-shaped faces aimed
at other prey. Deer ticks, clinging to thousands
of tall blades, prefer to jump their perches
for some piece of puppy ass, waving at the sky
in happy oblivion. And even the darkening sky,
with its strong, broad shoulders,
seems interested in other things.

When My Monster Finally Appeared

I almost didn't recognize him. And because I'd imagined
the usual suspects, I'd overlooked the obvious threats.
My monster was no hockey-masked boy walking
toward me with a chainsaw. His face did not turn
green with the effort of spinning itself around.
He didn't stumble stupidly in relentless search
for living flesh. He made no moves on the dog,
on my sleeping children, on the heavy equipment
parked in the garage. When my monster finally
appeared, he spoke with a soft voice I thought I knew,
said things I might've found convincing on any other day.
He moved and breathed and smelled like someone I thought
I loved. And after the dishes were done and the kids were
watching television, he said *I have something to tell you.*

Tiger

She stops short of licking them,
though the impulse to nibble on them is strong,
like scent. She will manage them by turns
on her narrow back, find a way to feed them,
digging at the roots with claws, bleeding and black.
If need be, she will tear the face from every other living thing
with her strong white teeth, carry them with fangs so gently
they will think they are her own powerful arms
grown long and striped. She will lay them,
tucked into a depression in the ground
she digs herself and makes soft with leaves.

My own mother might have said, *You are good
enough already. Because I am your mother,
I will carry you on my back, tired as it is,
and lay you down in the darkness
to find your own way.*

I heard instead
the length of fingernails
the length of skirts
the length of hair
the length of time.
Right words. Right work. Right man. Right way.

Three on the Tree

I am fifteen when he teaches me how to drive. Turning my palm toward my face, with his hand on the back of mine, we pull it toward us and drop it down into first. The shift into second is the quietest—our hands resting on top, arcing toward the sky until it catches and I can ease out the clutch, pushing hard on the pedal a full foot off the floor. Left one up and right one down until they meet in the middle. Third is our reward, a hard drop down with no regrets, the truck gently rocking as we cover miles. He is right about so many things, I have some trouble keeping track. Needing help from time to time, I accept it without shame. Flat tires and an empty bank account, sick children and an ego kicked and low, losses in love beyond any words. Facing disaster, I think of long spring days with him beside me, my hands at 9 and 3 and Springsteen belting words of hope and failure.

Burn the Ships

Fearing his soldiers would choose the safety of what they knew
over the promise of what they didn't,

Cortés set all his mighty ships afire, stranding himself
and his men in unfriendly Veracruz.

It is a glorious story, much better than the anguished
truth: the mutiny uncovered, the sad scuttling

of the ships that sent them creaking into the sea,
no gorgeous blaze to mark their beautiful demise.

How he must have suffered. The bitter betrayal,
the unknown world he had yet to conquer.

When we burn our ships we want to picture them
ablaze behind us, the heat warming our necks

as we move from the crackling destruction.
Instead, there is only the sucking sound of sinking.

The Corpse of Memory

    for Adam Johnson

I believe they still use shock therapy
to snip the strings of memory
in some parts of the world.
Deep in a bunker in North Korea,

for instance, disloyal citizens are
unburdened of their memories
of childhood, children, parents, friends.
The magnolia loses its distinctive taste,

and the hungry belly forgets its grip
as blue tongues of shock lick the brain
in predictable intervals. Gray matter
jiggles loose from its moorings,

freeing the brain of those meddlesome
connections, tight tissues that bind
to things that have no value anymore.
If that doesn't work, there is always

lobotomy, performed simply with a straight,
sharp object like, say, a metal nail file
pounded in through the ocular cavity,
so efficient there is hardly any blood.

What if Emerson was wrong when he
told us to drop the corpse of memory?
The dust puffing upwards as our arms
hang slack and newly weightless?

Cutaway

I am not so young that I cannot see
what is happening here. Over sounds
of the dishwasher I hear voices.
My mother, asking the question over
and over again without heat or any real need
to hear him, sitting at the kitchen counter
with her book open maybe reading,
maybe not. My father, his head held low,
then lower still, circling behind her.
I hear her say more quietly
than I've ever heard her speak,
Just tell me, just tell me now.
And he says, *I have something to tell you.*

We watch an episode of *M*A*S*H* that I've seen
a dozen times, the one where Hawkeye
really loses it for good. He remembers
the Korean woman strangling a chicken on the bus
to keep it quiet. Sidney Friedman is called in
to dig deep, to uncover not a chicken but a baby.

My mother rushes from the bedroom where
she gathers me and my sister. She helps us
find our shoes, pushes us out the door, goes
back into the house to collect the guns.

Holding them carefully by the grips,
pointing them down like her father taught her,
she hands them over. I notice she has no shoes
on her feet, the red polish on her big toe is chipped.

OCD

Here in this room I want to control the dust

want to sweep my hand across every
        plane

until the grain is clear and reflects the
        light.

I want stiffly ironed sheets that feel like
        new

and though it's too dark outside to see, I
        want

clear windows that smell like vinegar. My
        boy,

asleep beside me in bed-clothes almost
        clean,

is not enough.

Washing Rice

Don't ever ask me where to buy the rice,
or what kind of rice to buy, or how many

times I think you should wash the rice
to remove the starch, or why you should

remove the starch at all. Don't speak to me
in cups of water, degrees, or minutes

it should take before the steam appears
and then subsides, showing you the rice

is ready to fork by sticky lumps
into your wide and hungry mouth.

Listen while I tell you how the grains
feel slipping between my fingers as I draw up

handful after handful from the bottom.
Whisper *what do you think about?* when I

part the rice from small streams of water
the color of breast milk. Gently ask how

swirling it with my fingers and feeling
the sturdiness of each grain makes me hold

my breath. Touch me and know how trapping
the rice with my hand at the bowl's lip

and tipping it far enough to drain the water
lets me expel my breath, whole

and sure enough to measure the water
with my hand alone.

I'll do all of this for as long as it takes the sun
to set above the trees outside our kitchen window.

You'll speak to me in new ways, or I'll tell you
nothing you want to hear.

Dangerous Rooms

They are a complex, slate-hard hive
of rooms shut tight with padlocks,
the kind we saw that spring walking
across Fort Duquesne Bridge holding hands.

What's in these rooms I should not say—
what I thought of you and of me
moldering with things once lovely.

Just outside you'll find the dark, pacing
movements of an animal grief.

Wishing Doll

He's squatted on the bookshelf for years,
hardly drawing dust on his crimson jacket,
even after weeks of neglect. Faithlessly
I've dusted him, felt the multitude of ridges

hardened from the paper and flour
he's formed from, fingered the depression
of his face that looks like an even bite
from an artificial apple. His painted

eyebrows form the hopeful wings of a crane,
and chop hairs, meant to look like tortoise shells,
are rushed and uneven, the shoddy work
of a quick-handed man cranking out

Daruma dolls at piece-work rate.
Looking toward the corner
of the room, catching the eyes
that seem to follow wherever I go,

I swear he sometimes winks at me.
Weighted at the bottom, my little man
will never fall over, will never lie
still and wait for it all to be over.

Seven times down and eight times up
is what the Japanese say, and I know this is
a metaphor for my life, for everyone's life.
The second eye, Sharpied in by the man I

once loved, makes me think I should set
my own goals, should pack my bags
and head to the other side of the world
where I can burn him up and start again.

When I Leave You

Don't look for obvious clues,
like the vague scent of alien aftershave
on the blouses I left in our closet.
You'll find no calls to a number you don't
recognize, or piles of oversized clothes
that don't fit me anymore. Good luck
rifling through the trash in search of
crumpled receipts to a restaurant
you never took me to. When I leave you,
look for gummy, flesh-colored globs
swollen fat by water. Those remnants
of your morning oatmeal gathered
at the bottom of the sink
will tell you why I'm gone.

Law-man

Holding the dog by one brown paw,
you looked like you were shaking hands—
old friends you never were.
The dog, new dead, held her head against

your thigh. She seemed at play except
for the angle of her lolling tongue
that looked like graying salmon. I watched you stroke
her ear between your finger and your thumb,

and I recalled a story from your working life,
when you'd picked up that drunk on 795.
No more than twenty, handcuffed and riding shotgun,
he'd hocked a good one tattooing the glass.

With three quick cracks the flashlight broke his knee.

I guess he's not the only one, though you
never talked about the others. I'd learned the lesson
that was meant for me. *Don't ever cross me.*

Would it have surprised those boys to see you here,
nose dripping into matted fur? That great brown body
cold and heavy on your lap?

I can see your bent frame still, leaning on that kennel
while you search for words. Some version of I'm sorry
no dead dog would hear.

Amnesty

All of her aunts and cousins, her mother and siblings
told her that mixing with whites
only comes to no good. But she left them
anyway, her suitcases aimed at another life.

In America, she thought the can of Crisco
was filled with fried chicken, and then
her in-laws brought her broken scissors
and bags full of oversized hand-me-downs.

Years afterward, she told me so much more,
smiling over drinks that were *Too strong!*
And in that restaurant with the good booths
where you can learn Italian while you pee,

                I forgave her.

What I Learned from William James

Coffee, strong and black,
is good for me.
The grass will grow slower
now that I've cut it short.
Clothes are clean and folded
and put away.
Humidity is a forgotten dream.
My body expels every toxin
it may have harbored.
(I won't tell you how I know.)
The children favor books over television.
My friends don't talk about me
behind my back.
Flossing means I'll keep my teeth,
and the dog is learning not to tear the carpet.

Self-help

First, get yourself a good cast iron pot. Don't skimp.
You know what kind; you see them everywhere
and think *Who would pay that much for a fucking pot?*
You will. Go to every Marshalls, TJ Maxx, and
Home Goods in a hundred mile radius, and maybe
you'll get lucky and find an odd colored one—
mustard yellow or baby shit brown—marked way down
because some people only care about how these things
look, not what they do. My aunt's like this.
Had a pantry full of every kind—grill pan, Dutch oven,
braiser, you name it. I don't think her manicured hand,
always holding a Virginia Slim, ever touched one.
Even if you don't find one cheap, get one.
Steal it if you have to. I won't judge.

Once you get your pot, you'll know why you have it.
This pot can do anything and perfectly, every time.
Fancy a fry up? You have your pot. Need a twenty minute
cry? You'll have a perfect risotto when it's over.
Want to make grand statements with a heavy thud
while you're tidying up? Turn to your pot. Soak it
for no longer than 30 minutes and you'll be able
to wipe whatever's stuck to it free with a soft sponge.
No need for a man to provide the elbow grease.

In old pictures of refugees, the ones that show women
with their bundles tied tight with string, there is always
a pot balanced on top of their precious possessions.
You'll never wonder again what it means.

Reconciliation

It's 4:37 in the morning and I am almost all here.
Listening for the heavy sound of the fan kicking on,
muffling the thuds of the delivery truck unloading fruit,
the rumbling, irregular traffic on Mill Road,
the inexplicable banging in the hallway which will
probably wake the dog and start him whining again,
I brace for your first touch. Always coming these days
just before daylight, always alighting on one of three places.
Staring at the circular stain on the ceiling, I see the inevitability
of your progress like I sense the sound of my own voice
from inside my head. Very soon, your arms will frame my
arms, my legs will gird your legs, and I will hear again
the words you also said to her. Wanting to tell you only things
that are true, I'll swallow my words as they come to me.

What I Learned from Ruby

It was Sunday and I was tired,
restless and unsettled in the bone-hard pew.
Just then I recognized her hair,
that tangled mess of brown she'd had
as a girl, now picked through with gray.
It had been twenty years since I'd seen her last,
but when she turned her face toward me
I knew that blink of blue, that ski-jump nose.
Her name was Ruby.
Red, the bright bold knoll of puberty,
the knife-blood red of childhood fresh gone.
Gone suddenly, not the whispered hush of change
that happens slowly, imperceptibly, like forgiveness.

I was fifteen when my father told me
what happened to Ruby and why she moved away.
He told me driving in the car, the way he told me
everything too difficult to face.

I thought of Ruby's father, his cigar-stained hands
impatient, folded over the steering wheel of their old car
while he waited at the bus stop in the blazing heat.
I thought of days when I'd ignored her because
she was dirty or I was tired of pretending
that she was my friend.

Here in God's house she offered me a sign of peace,
a polite smile bending her lips. Taking her warm hand
in mine, I sought forgiveness for my trespass,
for not knowing what I'd done.

When She Dies

Go shopping or fly to Aspen or dig yourself
a good deep hole to sit in while you wait for a rain
that will fill it with water until it covers your head
and you can hear your own heart beat again.
(You'll find the quiet a blessing in that cloudy place.)

When you are ready, pull yourself out of the cold water
and into the house so you can drown again between its warm walls,
silent and still as the dust collecting on the banisters.

Don't drive yourself anywhere.
Don't break the hand that's offered to you,
    squeezing tightly because you think it might change the outcome.
Don't look for her in someone else's face, seeking more of her
    in the breathing man or woman who takes down your information.
Do listen to the tall, handsome doctor who speaks
    with such authority.
Don't look too closely at your girl's face
    because she'll look like a stranger, bruised and bloated and still.

When your only child dies on a Wednesday afternoon
playing softball in the bright sun, her lovely hair
spilled into the sand that clings to it,
be sure to call your insurance agent, Bob, I think it is,
so he can tell you what to do next.

Take You Back

Just when I think I can live without you,
I hear the chirping of a smoke detector,
the sound a bitter reminder of a world
of men whose arms and legs are longer
and stronger than my own. I think of
neck-snapped mice in complex traps,
uncut weeds teeming with ticks,
cars with flat tires or one extinguished
headlamp winking at my incompetence.
That box too heavy to lift squats on the landing
of my inadequacy, and the plumbing
that drips into the early hours of the morning
sings to me in dulcet tones of forgiveness
that pave the way for your return
and the sound of your breathing beside me.

White

Instead, I spotted our mother in a tiny
chair in the back row, her blue-black head
shining unnaturally. She was dressed

in clothes she'd laid out in her mind
the day before, when her hands
were moving along spools of color,

bright rainbow of threads flying through
air as loud as a train. It cost her half a day's
piece-work to see her boy and girl out-read them all.

Her own English, bent and twisted still,
after all those years, carried whiffs of garlic and
fish sauce. We hoped she would be silent.

At home, where every night we waited for
the rice to steam, her soft chatter lulled us to sleep.

Secure-in-place

Driving home on an ordinary Wednesday you expect to hear
the catalog of familiar things: abc order, playground arguments,
then three times everything up to twelve. But terror drills
are something new, something that makes you pay attention
instead of rehearsing the grocery list in your head or organizing
the weekend into drop-offs and pick-ups, softball and ballet.
We had to hide and stay quiet while our teacher locked the door.
She's on her third chirping sentence before the words break
through and stop in your head, like someone's yanked up
the handle of the emergency brake. *Mrs. Kirby put a card
in the window so someone would find us.* And you listen closely
now, willing yourself to drive the posted speed limit, reminding
yourself to breathe. *Then Sr. Barbara made an announcement
and said the drill was over, that we could stop hiding.*

And while she moves on, you remember your bedroom
window, the sticker your father rubbed his fist across to make it stay.
You thought the sticker, black and red with metallic trim,
was pretty, and you begged for another to put on your toy box.
Your father had a look on his face you mistook for anger.

Now you imagine the picture that must have formed in his
brain all those years ago, the blaze and billows of black smoke,
strange men in masks and heavy boots breaking the window
to search for his child. Relieved you're facing forward so she
can't see your face made ugly by images of guns, of broken glass
and blood, you work to make sense of this new language.

Something New

The second time I married him, we planned it in an hour
instead of days. No music, no flowers, no agonizing search
for the blue velvet dress I wanted to wear instead of white.
This time I wore a light gray dress I rather like to wear
on Mondays, shoes that don't cripple me when I walk.

The second time I married him, I wasn't worried about
how we would pay for the new roof on our home. No thesis
to defend, no relationships to negotiate. My brother sat
beside his wife, not on a cot in Saudi Arabia waiting for
the sun to rise. Our children stood beside us, our son as tall as I.

The second time I married him, I didn't wonder if this marriage
would last forever. I didn't worry he would see me for who
I really am, wasn't afraid that he might leave me for a little
while, keeping company in his heart with someone else.
I said *I do*.

Heavier

You're right, I agreed to go. I followed you that morning
when the grass was frozen stiff under my boots.
I carried in my thin arms what you'd given me to carry:
a cardboard box filled with tin cans and the metal target.

Like lovers on an out-of-season picnic, we walked
until the hills around our home looked unfamiliar.
You carried the gun, a Ruger no bigger than my hand
which you liked to hold because it's small.

I saw the tree you'd described to me a dozen times,
its black trunk chipped and blasted raw, I saw
the creased, frozen mounds rising up behind it,
protecting the world from your strays.

You arranged the box, balancing the cans on top
and shoved the plinker into the ground to its right.
I thought, this is where you bring our son,
the boy it took me twenty hours and a pint

of dark blood to bring into this world.
It will make you feel better to see for yourself,
and to stop you from asking again I said yes.
You adjusted the vinyl cups around my ears,

carefully handed me the gun and racked it because
you knew my hand wasn't strong enough.
You know your son can do this by himself. I held
my breath and words and thought, how ludicrous,

the boy not old enough to drive, to shave, to kiss
a girl. You stood behind me, your legs framed my legs,
your arms girded my arms as I took aim, let out my
breath and pulled the trigger. Like the white hot pain

and glittering shock of my first time, the explosion
shook me hard, leaving me numb from more than
just the cold. I handed back the gun and walked
home heavier, though my hands were empty.

Glamour Moving

I could tell he didn't believe me when I said the man
and boy who booked the truck and four-man crew
were soon following me across the state line and into
a second home where we would begin new lives together.
I knew it from the way he scanned the items still left
in this house: the cluttered countertops and stand mixer,
the knives magnetized to the wall, the dish towels
still hanging on the oven handle. Taking stock of the boxes
I'd neatly pushed against the wall, of me, composed,
he wasn't buying it. His handsome face, creased by
the sun or a pack-a-day habit, betrayed a kind of pity
that made me fight the urge to reach for his hand,
to tell him everything will be ok. No one is falling
apart here. We're in this thing together.

Pre-op

I try sleeping on my back the whole night, and when I wake I think, do I know pig Latin? I make a cup of Earl Grey since the bergamot makes me sick. I pull on a sweater the color of applesauce, the one with sleeves just a little too long. I squeeze into a pair of scuffed loafers that pinch my feet in the tenderest places below my smallest toes. I wear no makeup but paint my nails a bright blue. Not wanting to give up books, I grab the paper. I pick the route with six traffic lights, all timed wrong. I go in through the out door and hop into a wheelchair, rolling backwards beside him. As the nurse takes his vitals, I crouch on the bed, gnawing the sheets. Once they take him away I invert myself against the wall in the waiting room, head on the floor and heels against the paint because people stand upright and I might have to again.

Meet the Faces

Arm swaddling a too-large pile of rumpled shirts
and pants, hangers squeezed under the other,
I push my way into the Korean dry cleaner.
Today I'm looking for a quick escape,
hoping I won't witness the kind of scene
I've come to expect here: a frustrated giant of a man
looming over the narrow counter toward
the tiny, dark woman behind it.
Hearing her bend her tongue around
the words like stones in her mouth,
I'll wrestle with what to do next.

Do I intervene? Do I show her
what I am? As a child I wouldn't have hesitated
to translate her English into a clearer English
I know this man will understand.

She is not my mother, though every word
she sputters is as clear to me as the words
my own mother spoke, slaughtered
vowels and garbled consonants.

Today I step inside the warm shop and there
is only the woman, staring at a small television
while she pedals a sewing machine.
"Rosy Lovers," the latest Korean drama,
grips her full attention.
I know this one: a boy and girl
conceal their love behind
unspoken courtesy.
I see the woman's face soften,
a smile bends her lips.
My arms tire, and as I edge
toward the counter, set down my load,
the hangers slip from my armpit
and clatter to the floor.
The woman jumps, rushes to the counter.

Once we conduct our brief business
she turns from me, her face a closed curtain.

Driving Home on a Cold Night after a Snow Storm

It's more than quiet, and you realize
that's because the children you always see
playing in the road by that dirty house
along your route are nowhere to be found,
their ugly playthings hidden under
fondant snow. It would be wrong to
call it peaceful, though the snow lies
still at the base of every wall, tidying
what it can, everywhere it touches.

You hope you will never see again that fat
boy laughing, their filthy dog foraging
in the trash, the broken bits of plastic life
piled high by the outbuildings near misspelled
signs in DayGlo paint warning us to keep away.

Just then a figure emerges from the side door,
cupping his hand to protect the flame. Afraid
of what you might see next, you drive
a little faster. In your rearview mirror you
see him standing stiller than the snow, an orange
tip glowing bright like the Christmas lights
someone thought enough to string.

News of the Day

Some were plain bad luck. That boy in Lewistown
who lost his arm in the thresher while his father
fed the cows. The mayhem, the riots and that
poor man pulled from his truck and beaten
senseless. Some were just accidents.

But what about that house down the street
with the peeling paint and those endless windows?
Those children with their hollow eyes?

He didn't tell us why they'd moved
or what happened to that weird old car the father drove
while his wife rode in the back. He didn't tell us
the boy, the one who grabbed at private parts,
hung himself in a jail cell in Arkansas.
And his pretty sisters? God knows.

How to Talk to Strangers

Wandering up and down the aisles of our local Ames,
fingering cheap plastic ladles and bright balls of yarn,
I hid from my mother between the rounders of stiff shirts
and polyester pants. Her mangled words, the way she
haggled kept me out of earshot of the clerks who
spoke to her like she was deaf. I spotted the girl
grinning at me over bins of paper plates between us.
When she moved closer I could see the clips at the ends
of her tight braids, the skin of her palms shades lighter
than the tops of her hands. She was the first black girl
I'd ever seen, and I thought she wanted to talk to me,
to ask my name and how old I was and where I went
to school. Instead, my mother grabbed my hand and we
were out the door and into the bright sunlight.

1985

We were supposed to buy them, just
for one day. Three girls and four

boys in khakis and polo shirts.
Girls pooled their money to buy

the cute one whose bangs
nearly covered his eyes.

Preppy high school auctioneers
hawked their wares with great gusto,

and our men, in good spirit,
sported chains made of paper,

red and blue rings pasted together.
The room was in riot

when I spotted Miss Miller,
my algebra teacher.

Her hands were clenched
and she was weeping. I asked

my friend, a boy with perfect
teeth, if he knew why.

On the Anniversary of Your Infidelity

Moving around the bed, stepping with delicate feet
on every uneven surface, he settles finally on a place
behind my knees, curling into a tight, breathing ball.
Soon he'll begin to snore, and on trips to the bathroom
or to the dresser where we've placed glasses of water
out of his reach, we will move gingerly, careful not to
hurt him with our clumsy bodies. To think I once
considered boiling him in the pot I use to make soup.
Because you love him, too, I thought I might just
gather him up in my arms, let him lick my eyelids
with his flypaper tongue, sniff his fertilizer smells
one last time before dropping him into the boiling water
and closing tight the lid. I got the idea from that film
I saw on my very first date. The boy who took me,
it turns out, was damaged, too, and I wonder if he ever
thinks back to the dark theater smelling of popcorn,
his hand gently resting on my knee as we watched
the girl find the empty rabbit cage just as Anne Archer
opens the pot. I should have known you can't watch
a thing like that and expect to live happily ever after.

Cow

Weeks like this one make me wonder how nice
it might be to be a cow just chewing, slowly moving
my jaws in clockwise angles. Frothing green trickles
between my teeth and at the drooping corners
of my single-minded mouth, I could lie down
and rest on legs not asked to move, except to
escape the winds and stinging rain that come up
from the south, sometimes. Or maybe I'd just
stand here, letting the water wash my tough hide,
brown rivers of yesterday's dirt rolling inevitably
down into the holes I'm standing in—
thinking of no one in particular.

Not for the Voice of God to Save Him

I wonder if this other Isaac, I mean
the younger boy who lives in my father-in-law's

condo complex in Fort Myers, has any friends?
His father, drunk or stoned in his apartment

all day, has no idea where the son wanders.
Out to the beach to throw shells at birds and waves,

past abandoned towels to gather wallets and shoes,
into the pool where he dives to the bottom

to see how long he can hold his breath
in the water's stinging silence.

The retired veterinarian befriends him.
They play shuffle-board and pick up trash

along the sidewalk. They put wax on the Audi TT
and let it dry too long in the sun before wiping it down.

Like the warm-blooded creatures he handled,
perhaps he'll spare this stray dog,

the one the good mothers pull their children from.
I see the boy's translucent eyes, half-hidden behind

the fringes of overlong hair, watching.

The Transitive Property

Glass building tucked between the galleria shopping mall and Legg Mason. The cherry wood desk and ergonomic chair. Armani suits and Via Spigas. Burberry cologne. The cool jazz piped in on an enviable sound system. Bonus checks. The silver Audi A8. Perfect white smiles. Drinks at 6 under blue-domed lights. The expense account. Svelte, pony-tailed women with Louis Vuitton bags that would cost him, today, a whole month's salary. Now in his corduroy blazer and graph paper shirt, he teaches boys and girls the transitive property. Walking up then down straight rows, he knows from their answers which ones didn't eat breakfast or slept in a car. *Trey missed school again,* he tells me at home. *I'm trying to help him, but I'm afraid I can't pass him this time.* Or maybe a + b doesn't always equal c, and not everything that counts can be counted.

Conditional Love

I'll only love you if you do just what I say
in just the way I tell you to. I can think of
a hundred things you might do to lose my
love, everything from leaving your dirty
dishes in the sink to failing your algebra test.
Don't forget to comb your hair in the back;
that cowlick might be the end of you
and me. Your smart mouth might undue
every thread between us, so keep it shut
when you're talking to me.
See that your clothes are presentable,
your shoes are clean, your nails immaculate.
When you choose a mate, be sure it's
someone I'll connect with, someone
I'll like and who'll like me better than
most people do. Don't ever question my
judgment, my integrity, my intentions.
I am your mother, after all.

Notification of Family, 3 a.m.

When my father was new to the job, the kind
that turns happy boys into different sorts of men,

he knocked at the door of a just-turned
widow, though she didn't know it yet.

Gut-braced for the signs of shock
that would come, the pink of her face

draining into her bathrobe, he knew just how to
catch her when her knees began to buckle.

She'd never fall backwards like they did
in the movies he'd watched as a kid.

Grasping her shoulders, he'd help her
sink down straight where she stood,

repeating the words he'd said already
in his head. But when the door swung in,

she looked him in the eye as he said his part.
I knew that son-of-a-bitch would kill himself

one day, she said, thanking him politely
before shutting the door. My father

stood still a full minute before turning to go.
Later, sitting in his car, he remembered

she'd paused to light her Camel
after opening the door.

Clean

> after Philip Levine

For our mother, who left the house
every morning at 5 a.m.,
her dark eyes bruised with sleep,
it was a life sentence.
We had no idea what she did
all day at the factory.
Homework and piano lessons,
baseball practice and the latest hairstyles
in *Tiger Beat*. Levi's rolled
just above the right shoes,
we never wondered what it cost
walking through those heavy doors
before the sun had broken through,
into a world scorched with noise and heat,
feeding a loom that was never full.

I was twelve and my brother,
one year older, signed us up
for the job without asking me.
Snipping stray strings
from the multicolored patches,
Red Sox, Boy Scouts, a barracks
full of policemen, the marines
slipped through clumsy fingers.
Boredom crouched in our brains
like ether.

From our corner of the world
we couldn't see the frenzied
movement of the piece-workers,
their worth measured in
units per minute.
We lasted three days,
but it was years before I
understood why she never
seemed happier than on
the day we quit.

Maybe Next Time

There's nothing wrong here,
the way they go about their days
while I tap at keys or retreat to my bed.

Racing to the woods to hunt
for speckled salamanders and spade foot
toads, they'll bob in and out of shredded

light, flanked by stout oaks
and paper birches, sycamores and pine.
They'll spot pink crayfish in silver streams

and look for fox babies
hidden under cool outcroppings
blanketed with lichen. Jumping from rock

to far rock, scaling sharp cliffs
with tight grips and hand boosts, they're
prey to deer ticks, poison ivy, and mosquitoes.

Molested by thorns, skin slippery
with humidity, they will carry in their small
hands long, sharp sticks to protect them, waving them

like swords and poking at the world
unfamiliar before today. When they come home
they will find me silent and standing at the window

sipping my second glass of Tanqueray,
which always tastes to me like pine cones.

Woodcutting

When the air finally turns, gripping invisible droplets of water so tightly it hurts to breathe, I know they'll say it's time to cut more wood. By now I've memorized their movements: how they'll clean and oil the chainsaw until its little engine heart stops skipping, choose the boots with the hardest toes, gather their gloves and wedges, and set out for the woodline where so many trees have fallen already. I'll listen for a break in the buzzing rhythm, prepare myself for the terrible sounds that signal there is no going back, that some things done or said are irrevocable. Remembering the sad man who bought my childhood home, the one who split his foot in half with an ax, I don't need to tell you it's not the worst thing that could happen. Years before, bending to retrieve a dropped book, his little boy was killed by the school bus as his sister waved goodbye to her friends. They called the father at the cement factory to tell him. Once I thought there could be nothing worse than chopping off your foot, your own bright blood pulsing out around you, the ugliness of torn flesh, your sweat smelling of fear. Today I wonder what he was thinking when he did it. *Now, this?* Or was he grateful for the thud of pain, for knowing that what just happened might just happen to any man chopping wood. That somehow, you could prepare for things.

Zoonosis

There is no end to the dangers animals pose.
Microscopic deer ticks have the indecency
to leave behind swollen joints, fever

and fatigue after sucking our blood.
Neglected dogs and ordinary raccoons
become bewildered malcontents,

appearing in strange habitats, snapping
at us with their foaming jaws.
And those innocent cows, munching

away in patty-smeared fields, contaminate
our boots and swell our brains.
Instead, what if we passed our crippling

maladies to our animal friends?
When we stroke their backs and scratch
behind their ears, feeling along the tender

depressions in their skulls, what if we infested
them with anxieties, with depression inked in
deepest blue? Suppose we splashed our

traumatic memories in Technicolor across
their innocent brains, paralyzing their senses?
What if, unwittingly, we infected an army

of mosquitoes with our control issues?
Swarming in unison, they would look for ways
to call the shots for every living thing.

Imagine the damage that we'd do.

Wait for It

Lying on his belly on the hot wooden
planks, arms extended over the edge,
he looks a little like a crab himself,

white arms and legs splayed for balance.
I watch him hoist by inches the hand line
he hopes will draw a crab to the surface,

its claw locked onto the gray bubbled skin
of the chicken neck he tied to the end
of the string, an ugly watch on the end

of its fob. When he spots the crab,
its belly exposing the finger-thin apron
of a large male, he steadies the hand line

just above the water as he reaches
for the net with his right hand. Arcing wide
and low, he steadies the mouth of the net

below the crab just as it senses
the deal's gone bad, opening its dactyl
to drop the loot. Measuring the spine

from thumb to pinky, careful to avoid
its claws, the boy grins when he sees
that it's a keeper. Later, as he's snapping off

its pereopods to suck at their hinges, cracking open
the propodus so he can dig at the meat,
I shudder at this creature I couldn't have made.

I'll Take Your Jacket When You Die

I know how this happened.
The tradition of naming things
one might pass on to loved ones
got him thinking about his share.

I mentioned a keepsake,
a ring or a piece of furniture
that would be mine or my husband's
when some elder relative passed away.

I'll take your jacket when you die.

It's not like I think he'll be crouching
behind the pie table, plotting.
But the indifference of his
ten-year-old heart unhinged me
and I tasted fear.

Any Dog Will Bite

Any dog will bite is one of those
things my father says
from time to time. I know
he means to teach me lessons
until they sink in, like the teeth
of that snapping mongrel he sees
in his head, the dog a stand-in
for everything he fears
or thinks I should.

Out my kitchen window I see
our son, sitting still on the bank
behind our house. His shoulders
curl forward like a question mark
as he props his elbows
on his knees. The gun,
which looks to me like a real gun,
shoots small plastic pellets
from an orange tip. He stares
unblinking through the sights
arranged on the barrel,
the pink tip of his tongue
exploring his upper lip.
He squeezes the trigger,
nailing the paper target twenty
yards away. Over and over
he reloads and fires, making
tiny adjustments that improve
his aim. I can almost feel
the clicking of good gears
in his eleven-year-old head,
can almost smell the concentration
in his boy fingers. From here
I can only see the side of his face,
shining with triumph or
maybe something more.

It's No Wonder We Never Learned to Swim

It was hard to focus with her standing there,
the other mothers off smoking Benson & Hedges.
No wonder our thin arms and legs could never do
what those tanned teenagers wanted them to do.
Breaststroke, butterfly, backstroke, the crawl
eluded us, our faces cocked toward the boundary
where our mother stood unmoving.
Her long, lovely fingers locked around
the chained link, her white palms dry and stiff
as gruesome monkey paws.
Lord knows she had reasons enough:
a drowned-at-seventeen brother, for one.
But faced with that choking blue,
we wished she'd kept them to herself.

Chink

In the fourth grade Billy Morton calls me a chink and at first I think it's because he sees my mother sitting quietly in the last row behind all the other mothers on back-to-school night, her black-ink hair down to her waist, a curtain to everyone whenever she bends her head, but Billy Morton is always watching Kung Fu and even though David Carradine doesn't look Chinese and isn't supposed to, people call him "chink" and Billy Morton wants to try it out on his own tongue, to push it forward with his breath, to feel how it tastes leaving his mouth, and I love words too so I say *you're a chink* and his face folds in on itself and he starts to cry and Sister Regina points her long witch-bone at me all blue in the face *Do you know what that means?* and I say no but I know what it means it means I can make you cry any time I want.

Bad Day

A boy with thick hands
stumbles into her room
where she's been reading.
His head on the side of her bed,
sobs shaking his frame in electrified jolts,
he recounts his day.

She sees that he is sweating
and his eyes are swollen with disaster.
This mother, who means to console him,
puts down her book and glasses
and tells him he'll suffer greater losses.

> *You will never be a professional athlete.*
>
> *Someone you love will not love you back.*
>
> *Your dog will die.*

Standing in the doorway,
the father asks quietly why she does this.

> *I'm giving him the world.*

Loaner

I'm after blue socks, those gray, pilled trousers,
that shirt with the broken corozo buttons.
I finger a toothbrush, test the tweezers,
run my hand along the smooth edges
of cheap frames. Silently shifting a figurine
of a boy and girl playing leap frog in their Sunday best,
I wipe dust from silk flowers, step closer to the bed,
bury my face in the bend of the blanket,
sniff its coldness until I locate their scent,
freshest in these folds. I must not linger,
must not run my hands over dusty things,
the dear detritus of dead parents.
Sometimes that man, that boy and girl
seem like a temporary arrangement.

A Love Story

when you have forgotten Sunday: the love story
—Gwendolyn Brooks

I want the sniffling boy I'm eyeing in the public library to feel hugged, though he doesn't know me and I wouldn't dare touch him as I slip by. Hunched over his paperback, upper teeth locking bottom lip firmly in place, my new boy is a study in concentration, vertical lines separating plain, upturned brows, a dignified jut to a jaw already looking old. Brown eyes never leave the page while he folds his spent gum in a wrapper and scans the lines for zombies, aliens or robots on this Sunday evening of screaming sirens and faded yellow light. There is no such thing as no-expectation.

Mother

Last night I dreamed you were a small black bear
come to me from an
unknown place. No one

else recognized you, but I would know
the deep set of your
round bright eyes anywhere

no matter that your bear's eyes were brown,
not light blue. You held
me tight with your thick

bear arms, right around the middle where
you used to hold me
when you were small.

You took my hand in your paw to show me
what you'd like to eat,
bright things in crinkly papers,

and I said *no* as gently as I could.
You eat this apple
I've quartered, or

this peach. After wiping your maw I said
Let's play nicely with
these boys and girls. No

kicking or biting, bear. Be nice. Next I
showed you how to write
your name in big

broad letters, and you wrote them clearly
so the others could
read them without my

help. We did these things again and again
until you grew tired
and rubbed your eyes. I

put you to bed, stroking your ear until
you closed your eyes and
your mouth fell open,

exposing crooked rows of sharp white teeth.
They told me I was
crazy, whispered lies

about my little bear. *He will not hurt
anyone*, I said,
almost believing

it myself. Studying your long thick claws,
I thought maybe I'd
just chew them down while

you slept, little bear, just like I did when
you were a baby
and had fingernails

like paper.

Go There

Why is it my responsibility? he's thinking, and I know I'll have to work harder, find a better way to make him understand who I want him to be, who I want every boy to be. *But if I don't get in trouble, isn't that good enough?* And I look at my 15-year-old grown taller and stronger than I ever imagined him, find his pale blue eyes nearly hidden under camel lashes, my forehead barely reaching his chin. "Come and look," I say, trying to temper the desperation I feel, pointing to the digital pictures on CNN, the mugshot of a different almost-man with light hair and bloodshot eyes, pictures of the good Samaritans who climbed off their bikes to help the unconscious girl. I move through the narrative, explain everything that happened before, the too-light sentence handed down after. He looks over my shoulder, seemingly impassive. A hundred lessons I've taught him since he first breathed air, each one more important than the last. Casting about for words, feeling the urgency like someone's running up behind me, I speak the thought I can barely formulate. "What if that had been your sister?" I see the filament flicker in the center of his right eye, and I hear him breathe the word softly, without irony or impatience. *OK.* And I think, we're OK.

Acknowlegments

I wish to thank Tom Lombardo for choosing my book as the winner of the 2017 Press 53 Award for Poetry. I am deeply appreciative of the effort that Tom and Press 53 have put into my words. I also wish to thank Martha Collins for her generous help in editing the manuscript and for her belief in the book. I am grateful to my workshop teachers and friends at Bread Loaf, Colrain, Gettysburg, Southampton, and the Provincetown Fine Arts Center. I thank Mount St. Mary's University and all my good friends there. For their help in work and in life, I thank Tom Bligh, Lynn Rosas, Christine McCauslin, Mindy Korol, Dana Ward, and Tracy Koch. My deepest thanks goes to Grant Disharoon, who knows why.

Leona Sevick is provost at Bridgewater College in Virginia. Her work appears in *The Journal, Barrow Street, Potomac Review, North American Review, The Florida Review, Little Patuxent Review*, and in the anthologies *All We Can Hold: Poems of Motherhood* (Sage Hill Press, 2016), *Circe's Lament: Anthology of Wild Women Poetry* (Accents Publishing, 2016), and *The Golden Shovel Anthology: New Poems Honoring Gwendolyn Brooks* (Univ. of Arkansas Press, 2017). She is the 2012 first place winner of the Split This Rock poetry contest, judged by Naomi Shihab Nye, and a finalist for the 2016 John Ciardi Prize for Poetry. Her chapbook, *Damaged Little Creatures*, was published in 2015 by FutureCycle Press, which you can find at www.leonasevick.com

www.ingramcontent.com/pod-product-compliance
Lightning Source LLC
LaVergne TN
LVHW041345080426
835512LV00006B/625